'Dad... dad... dad...there's a HUGE hole in the ground and some people with hammers are looking into it...

Mum, why, mum?

Mum — they said they're 'ologists. What's an 'ologist mum?

What are they doi

Why?

Rocky is quite right. If there is a HUGE hole in the landscape — in a field — like a quarry — maybe 'ologists are looking into it.

Probably field geologists making a map, or hydrogeologists looking for water, or palaeontologists looking for fossils — or engineering geologists who want to build a dam, a bridge or a house.

They could be geochemists if they want to know what secrets are hidden under their feet.

They could even be palaeoentomologists — looking for ancient bugs and beetles.

Whatever they are, Rocky can be sure that 'ologists at work can be spotted... and geologists are among Nature's very own detectives. Rocky liked the idea of being another Sherlock Holmes but what sort of clues are 'ologists looking for... and where are they found... and do they have to dress up or use any special equipment for their work?

Rocky soon realised that almost everything in the world has something to do with geology. The paper this book is printed on and the ink that makes the words have something to do with geology. Every mountain and river, every ripple in the landscape and every road or railway, village, town and city have something to do with geology.

In this book we use very special ways of measuring, for example

1DDb = one double decker bus
1GBh = great big hole, or one football pitch
1 yonk = 40 million years (earth's crust became solid 100 yonks ago; the film Jurassic Park was set 2 yonks ago)

Rocky thought about being a geologist. 'The clues I have to look for are everywhere and in everything,' Rocky realised 'but the only equipment I need is a hand-lens — to see everything at a great magnification — and a hammer in order to collect small fragments of rocks, minerals or fossils... but I must wear a special pair of safety specs — to protect my eyes from flying chips of rock'

Now Rocky was ready to become a geologist and look for clues that would amaze everyone. 'Geology is for me!' Rocky thought. 'Not just for boring old people in dusty old rooms.' Rocky had seen 'ologists at work and they looked normal enough — but why were they peering into holes?

Eager to find out, Rocky put the equipment in a backpack and added a notebook and pencil.

I've only got
one set of eyes
That's all there'll ever be
If I take care of
them perhaps
They will take care of me

ROCKY

I want to grow up safe...

'To write down everything I see and hear' Rocky thought, 'and any long words that will need explaining later.'

'All I need now,' thought Rocky, 'Is a hole. Preferably a HUGE hole.'

But huge holes are rarely found where young people live. Rocky would have to settle for a smaller, safer hole to begin the exciting business of exploring an 'ology.

'I know! I can begin my investigations (good word, investigations) where my new house is being built. I must be careful, though, and make sure an adult is with me all the time.'

key point:
The stability of the house depends on the stability of the land on which it is built

Natural hazards

Folds and fractures happen when the crust moves.

Solution cavities are holes in the ground, usually in limestone and gypsum, where the rock has dissolved away and left a space.

Some kinds of rock like clay shrink, swell or slide downhill under the weight of a building.

Chemicals in some rocks, such as sulphates, damage concrete foundations.

So, hammer, hand-lens and notebook at the ready, Rocky went back to where the new house was being built. Rocky realised that earlier on, before the first bricks were laid down, engineers and perhaps a geologist came to make sure it was a safe place to build.

They had to find out what was underneath the surface. They also had to be sure that the ground was strong enough to hold the weight of all the houses on the new estate.

Sometimes there are old, underground mine workings which could give way and cause walls to crack or houses to collapse, into big holes that could be a DDb deep. This is called subsidence. Rocky wrote it in the notebook. A copy of a page of Rocky's book is on the back page of *this* book.

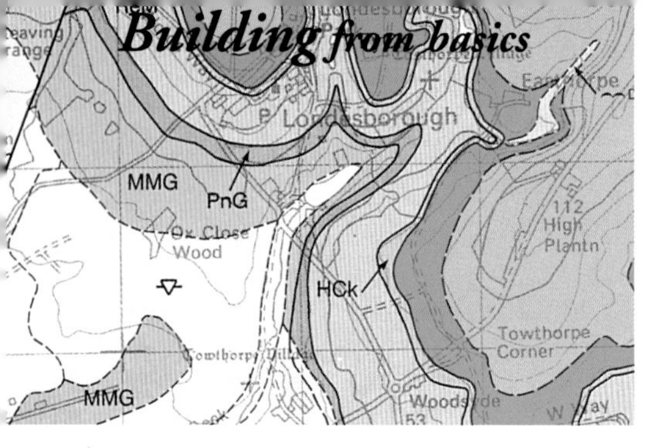

Snippet of a geological map.

Geologists must be sure that no dangerous gases are coming out of the ground. There are gases, like radon, which are quite normal and natural but which can be dangerous if too much is allowed to build up inside a home.

Other gases, like methane, can come from rocks rich in carbon or decaying rubbish.

...if the geology is complicated.

Methane can explode, damaging people and property.

So it is either taken away or used as a source of natural energy. Read about renewable energy on page 16.

There are special maps called geological maps which Rocky thought were very clever. Like Ordnance Survey maps, they have contours (lines of equal height above sea-level) and show the positions of the roads, railways and all the villages, towns, cities and even isolated houses. But they are also coloured in like a painting to show where all the rocks are, even if you cannot see some of them. So how does a geologist know where they are and what they are?

When Rocky had seen the 'ologists they had been looking into a hole so perhaps that was the answer.

The British Geological Survey has a warehouse full of cores, hundreds and thousands of them from all over the British Isles. Many are of rocks dozens of yonks old — almost as old as Earth itself — and some of them are from very deep down, several DDbs in fact.

There are cores from the sea bed that were taken when they planned the Channel Tunnel, or from the North Sea before they found oil and gas. There are also lots of different machines and people that examine these cores and explain what the rocks mean.

All the information is called data. Data are kept on a computer programme called a database, which is a bit like an encyclopedia.

The rocks were hidden under the soil and the hole was like a window opening into the Earth's surface.

Man-made hazards include:

- Old mine shafts.
- Underground workings like those for limestone, salt or coal.
- Old quarries filled with rubbish from homes and factories. These are called landfill sites.

I want to live HERE!

Rocky already knew that when the geology was complicated, geologists drilled boreholes. The rock they take out, called a 'core', looks like a cork coming out of a bottle.

People have always needed rocks — and the rocks were here long before people were. People lived in caves, to protect them from the weather and wild animals, until they began wanting to live in places they chose — in villages and near their farms or water supplies.

Then people had to bring the rocks to where they wanted to live. They used stone tools to make houses from wood and grass. After a long time they began to use their tools to shape stones and, from then on, building stones became available.

They needed to find rocks that could be shaped easily, like sedimentary rocks. These are made up of fragments of other rocks, like sand on a beach or pebbles in a stream. One example of a sedimentary rock is sandstone which is widely used in building.

Rocky's piece of land is safe so a builder comes to carry out the first part of the work.

First the 'mains' are put in - these are the sewers and drains that collect used water and send it away for cleaning and recycling. The sewers carry waste water from toilets and sinks. The drains take away rain water.

The pipes used to be made of glazed stoneware or cooked clay and looked like long plant-pots. Later on, clay or concrete (see page 8) was used. You might see either of these pipes under old houses. These days, plastic pipes are used to carry water as well as gas supplies to the house (read about plastic on page 21).

The next job is to make roadways. These don't look like ordinary roads yet, but are just layers of sand and gravel called aggregate, lined with concrete kerbstones. Pipes and cables for the mains water, gas, electricity and telephones are laid down beside the road before dividing to reach each building plot.

The limestone belt

Amongst the many outstanding examples of the use of local stone are those buildings built of Bath, Portland and Cotswold Stone.

These easily worked building stones were taken from a belt of Jurassic limestones that were deposited in seas about four yonks ago. The belt extends diagonally across England from the cliffs of Yorkshire to Dorset.

These limestones have always been thought of as special because they are easily shaped and 'weather' to a warm, cream colour. They have been used for building many of the colleges at Oxford and Cambridge Universities, civic centres, some of the finest country houses as well as whole villages in the Cotswolds. Without these limestones, which are often studded with the fossil shells of extinct sea creatures, the architecture of Britain would be deprived of some of its finest buildings.

Gradually, however, the 'good' limestone became expensive to quarry and another material, first used in the ancient city of Babylon some 6000 years ago, came back into fashion.

That material was brick (see above), one of the most adaptable of all building materials and cheaper than natural stone. Read about bricks on page 8.

Limestone cliffs, Yorkshire.

This is the time when individual houses are surveyed and their foundations outlined in lime.

Houses are built on foundations that help carry the weight of the structure and make sure that everything remains stable. In most of today's houses, the foundations are as deep as Rocky is tall and hold enough concrete to fill a swimming pool.

The whole area is flattened and covered with a layer of 'site concrete', to prevent damp coming up from the ground and stop plants growing under the floor. Rising damp can be a serious problem and houses have a damp-proof course to stop damp creeping up the walls and ruining the home.

In the past, damp-proof courses at ground level were made from tar, stone or metals like sheets of lead, copper or zinc. Special blue bricks or plastic sheets are used for this purpose today.

Rocky's house will be built of brick but some houses are built of natural stone.

The best kinds of rock for building can be cut in one or more directions and easily shaped.

What will my house be built of?

'I remember that sort of rock' thought Rocky. 'It is called *sedimentary.*'

Sedimentary rocks are quite soft and are usually 'banded' or layered like a sandwich. This is because they are formed from many different materials over a very long period of time. They can be separated into these layers and used in slices.

The second kind of rock is an *igneous* rock, an example of which is granite. The name comes from the Latin word meaning fire. 'It's a word-clue,' Rocky thought. 'It must mean that they were originally very hot.' Rocky was right, they were very hot but then they slowly cooled into a solid, crystalline form. They are often very beautiful and catch the light to twinkle in the sunshine.

A crystalline igneous rock.

Sandstone — a sedimentary rock.

The third kind of rock is called *metamorphic* rock because it has been changed either by heating up or squashing in the earth's crust. One example is slate. Slate was originally a black mud laid down on the sea bottom. Fossils can be found in it but they are often squashed.

Another *metamorphic* rock is marble which comes from limestone and is so beautiful that some of the world's most wonderful statues are carved from it.

Michelangelo, the famous Italian sculptor, used to say that he saw the figure inside the block of marble and all he had to do was cut away the stone that surrounded it. He believed (nearly but not quite) that wonderful statues were hidden inside marble like baby chicks inside eggs... waiting to be 'hatched' by his genius.

A banded metamorphic rock.

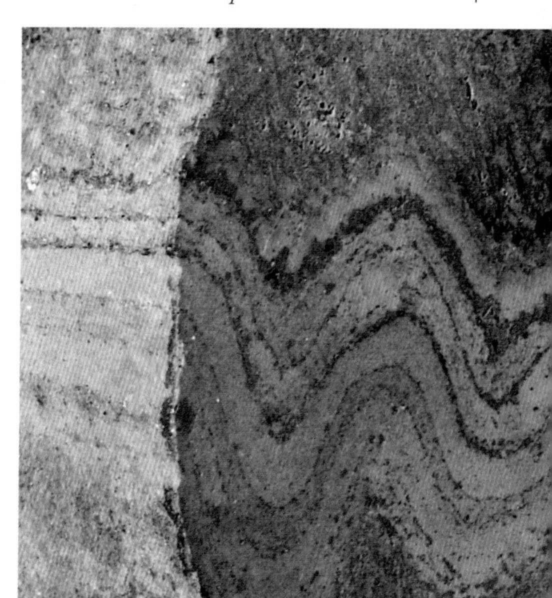

Clays suitable for brick-making

Clays are sedimentary rocks laid down under quiet water conditions like deep-water seas.
You can tell where brick clay is found because industries have grown up to use it for making pottery and bricks.
Look for brick kilns and their tall chimney stacks.

Flat-lying valleys in clay rocks.

But, like we said, Rocky's house will be built of brick. There are a lot of different bricks used in Britain, made from different kinds of clay.

The different clays, together with different ways of firing and shaping, produces a choice of bricks that range in colour from off-white and shades of cream, brown and red to nearly black.

There are also special bricks like firebricks used to line chimney shafts, boilers and kilns.

Rocky has seen the builders using breeze blocks — great big white blocks with hollow middles. These are made from cement and the ashes (or breeze) left behind in furnaces. They are cheap and useful for building quickly, if the wall is to be 'faced' or hidden behind a screen of good bricks.

Breeze blocks are cheap and useful if you're in a hurry.

Concrete, mortars and plasters

Concrete is essential these days. It is made by mixing cement (a mixture of chalk or limestone and clay) with sand and gravel or crushed rock (aggregates). Other important 'ingredients' in the construction of a house are:

- lime, also made from chalk or limestone and used in mortars and plasters, and
- gypsum (calcium sulphate) which is used to make plaster, plasterboard and cement.

What else goes into building my house?

The roof

Rocky's house will have a roof made from either slate or tiles.

Slate is formed from mud or a mixture of mud and ash poured out by ancient volcanoes and then changed by heat or pressure.

GREEN NOTE

In coal-fired power stations, sulphur dioxide is removed from the flue gases using limestone — which is converted into gypsum.

This process reduces acid rain and supplements the use of conventional gypsum.

'I remember metamorphic rock' Rocky thought, and checked to make sure it was written in the notebook.

Some other rocks, like sandstone and limestone, can also be found in thin layers. Cut up and left out in the rain to 'weather', they are used as a roofing material in many villages in eastern England.

Real slate and slices of limestone are expensive and difficult to find so, for Rocky's house, the builders have decided to use tiles.

Asbestos

Asbestos was once used for cheap roofing.

It is useful in some places because it doesn't catch fire.

But asbestos dust is bad for your health so it is no longer used.

Tiles are made from clay and baked in kilns. They could have chosen concrete mixed with sand and ash and coloured with a pigment, often iron oxide.

Slates

North Wales, Cornwall, the Lake District, Scotland (Ballachulish) and Ireland (Kilkenny) have good supplies of slate.

In Britain, the best slates are between 435 and 570 million years old — at least 11 yonks.

Aggregates

Aggregates come from man-made pits, river beds or the sea bed. They can be used to line roads (page 5) or mixed with cement to make concrete.

They need to be washed before use to get rid of anything that might spoil the cement.

There are gravel quarries which, when they are finished and filled with water, become nature reserves or watersport facilities.

Without quarries we might not have these facilities... it costs too much just to dig a big hole and throw away the rocks.

What else can old quarries be used for?

To be sure that the roof is weatherproof, the builder will put a thick blanket of fibre under the tiles. This blanket has been treated with bitumen — made from oil and coal — to keep out the rain.

The builder used something similar, with a crust of rock chippings, to protect the flat roof on the garden shed. But his friend used another bit of geology on his shed — he used corrugated iron — which is a very good material for roofs — until it rains, when it becomes too noisy.

Working quarry, Derbyshire.

Recreational use of a quarry in sand and gravel.

Corrigated iron is good until it rains!

Glass — sheets of liquid geology

Just before the roof is completed, the windows are put in. Their frames are usually made of wood, metal or plastic. Sheets of glass can be either *transparent* (see-through) or *translucent* (you can see light but not individual items through it).

Glass is made by melting a special sort of sand consisting of the mineral *quartz* or *silica*. In Britain, one of the sources of this silica-rich sand is Cheshire. Most glass used to make windows and bottles is made by mixing the sand with soda ash and lime. However, other chemicals can be added to produce different kinds of glassware.

What can be added to glass?

Heat-resistant glass — *alumina, silica, borax*
Coloured glass — *copper, gold etc.*
Heavy glass — *lead and barium oxide*
Cloudy glass — *fluoride or phosphate*
Sparkling glass — *oxides of lead, barium etc.*

Lead and glass

Lead is a grey coloured metal which feels very heavy — compared with other metallic elements. It is soft and easy to hammer and bend into shape. Leaded windows in churches and ancient buildings are a very visible use of this geological material. In the past, lead was also squashed through tubes (extruded) as gutters and downpipes and often stamped with the date of the property.

Courtesy of the Trustees of the Victoria and Albert Museum.

Insulation

Insulation is important to keep the warmth in and the cold or noises out of a house.

In the loft, the material is usually a mineral-wool fibre (made of melted rock or glass fibre) or vermiculite, a micaceous mineral that looks like flakes of skin.

If you ever use these minerals, be careful to wear gloves and knee pads — they are horrible to get on your skin.

A very lightweight material, which looks like hard white foam, is also used. Called expanded polystyrene, it is made from oil and is important for lagging water tanks, pipes and for filling in spaces in the walls.

Strips of plastic sponge are used as draught excluders around doors and windows. Bronze strips can be used down the sides of a door, because it is hard-wearing (bronze is a mixture of copper with tin).

Rocky's house is now ready to have the insides fitted.

Water, electricity and gas pipes, using mostly copper and plastic, are fixed before the walls are covered with plaster.

'I remember what plaster is made of' thought Rocky. 'It is made from *lime* and *gypsum* (*calcium sulphate).*'

Mineral-wool fibre in a cavity wall

Where does my tapwater come from?

In Britain the Chalk (shown here) is the most important aquifer but sandstones also play a significant role and one third of all water used in England and Wales is taken from aquifers. Water is taken out by pumps, like the one in the picture, and is piped to the towns.

Rocky's water will come from wells, through pipes deep in the ground.

Do you know where your water comes from?

Every day Rocky uses between 150 and 500 litres (30–100 gallons) of water. It is used for drinking, washing, flushing the lavatory, cooking and even, if essential, bathing.

Everywhere you look there are people washing cars and watering gardens and leaving taps running. But most people only notice water when they can't have it — during a very hot summer, for example.

Most of the rain or snow that falls either evaporates, is soaked up by the soil and plants or runs directly into rivers or lakes. Some sinks down, through tiny holes and cracks, into rocks which act as underground storage reservoirs.

These huge rock 'sponges' are called *aquifers* and the water stored there is known as groundwater.

In an aquifer, the level that the water reaches is called the *water table.* Water, as you can see in your bath, will find its own level. This happens underground, too. The water table moves up and down according to how much water is available to fill the given space... just like your bath water.

All holes in the ground act like wells and, if they go deep enough, will fill up to the level of the water table.

All holes in the ground think they are wells... if they are deep enough.

Some places get their water supplies from rivers that are filled up from groundwater.

However, what happens in areas where there are no aquifers either to supply wells or fill rivers? Some rocks (called *impermeable)* will not let water pass through them.

In such areas — including large parts of Scotland, Wales and the north of England — an artificial lake or reservoir has to be made. This is done by blocking a valley and catching the water of all the streams flowing into it.

Wherever it comes from, your water will be clean enough to drink. Groundwater is cleaned naturally as it moves slowly through tiny holes and cracks in the rock.

'But there are lumps of grit in my kettle'

All our water is checked by chemists and engineers employed by the regional water companies, to be quite sure it is safe to drink.

Different parts of the country have hard or soft water depending on the rocks in which the water is held. In a hard water area, Rocky could easily find gritty bits in the kettle. These are flakes of calcium or magnesium minerals that break away when a kettle has furred up.

Tiny amounts of mineral, originally from the host rock and dissolved in the water will make the water hard or even milky. Hard water is harder to make bubbles with. On the other hand, soft water comes from areas where there are metamorphic and igneous rocks, such as Scotland and Wales. Soft water makes a terrific froth with soap.

Reservoirs

Geologists have an important job to do when reservoirs are built. They must find suitable building materials and make sure that the dam is built on strong foundations so that it will not move (as in the illustration here) or fall over when subjected to the enormous water pressures.

'I bet I know why' thought Rocky. 'The different rock types mean that different amounts of minerals are dissolved in the water.'

'Is my water old?'

Yes. It could be a hundred years since your water fell as rain. Parts of Africa that have almost no rain at all have what is called 'fossil' groundwater that was trapped in the rocks thousands of years ago.

Water in aquifers is not as easily polluted as rivers or lakes, but it can still be made unfit to drink.

Fertilisers and pesticides used by farmers can get into groundwater through the rocks.

So can chemicals and fuels from pipelines and storage tanks which are accidentally spilled. Poisonous chemicals can leak from rubbish dumps.

Have you ever wondered what happens when a tanker has an accident and the Fire Brigade washes all the chemicals away?

They go into the drains and, sometimes, into the ground. Even the land next to motorways can get poisoned when the rain washes all the mess off the roads.

Groundwater stays in an aquifer for so long that we have to be very careful to protect the water that gets in there in the first place — and we check it very carefully when it comes out.

I want ENERGY!

Energy from the sun

Rocky's new house will use the energy of the sun. The builder has installed special windows called solar panels in the roof. These will absorb the sun's rays and convert them into heat and electricity.

Getting to the point

But most of the energy in the new house will come from power points that link cables carrying electricity around the house. Electricity comes from power stations across the country which transmit energy through a network of cables that go underground or are carried on pylons which stalk the countryside

Some energy sources that produce electricity and burn fossil fuels such as oil, coal and gas are non-renewable. Other sources are renewable — like hydroelectric or water power and wind power.

Hot rocks

Sometimes the earth itself produces enough heat to form an energy resource. This is called geothermal energy (from 'geo' meaning 'earth' and 'thermal' meaning 'hot').

Rocks are heated up by being buried deep down in the earth's crust where temperatures increase, mainly by the radioactive decay of minerals within the rocks. Heat also comes from the centre of the earth. These hot rocks, if they are wet, produce steam which, when it reaches the earth's surface, can be converted into electricity by a generator.

There are five basic sources of electricity

- *solar energy from the sun*
- *harnessing the elements — like wind and seas*
- *geothermal energy*
- *burning fossil fuels — like oil, coal or gas in power stations*
- *nuclear fission*

Some places, like Kenya (in Africa) have enough geothermal energy available to provide electricity for everyone in the country.

Alternatively, cold water can be pumped into hot rocks, like granites, to create hot water and after that, steam.

Steam can also be produced from energy released by the *nuclear fission* (or splitting of atoms) of elements such as uranium which comes from the ore *pitchblende*.

Bringing energy home

Electricity is brought to our homes by wires and cables made of copper.

Copper conducts heat and electricity better than any other known metal except silver and is present in every plug, socket, terminal point and micro-circuit in the house.

When the copper that brings electricity into the house is linked — using a plug — to the machine Rocky wants to use, a circuit is made and the power can get from one to the other.

Other energy

Oil, gas and coal are energy sources in their own right, as well as being used to make electricity.

There is more coal than any of the other three major fuels. In Britain, coal was formed hundreds of millions of years ago from the squashed remains of tree-filled swamps. It is found in layers (like a cake) between a few millimetres and several metres thick.

Steam generates energy.

Oil be seeing you

Rocky's home has an oil-burning stove. Oil is an important fuel (petrol comes from it) but it is also a lubricant, like the cans of oil and grease.

Plastic is made from oil. Oil is also used when making cosmetics, paints, medicines, pesticides and fertiliser. Imagine what your house would be like without oil. There would be no shaving cream and hair shampoo in the bathroom; no compact discs or videos. Not even a shower curtain. What else would be missing?

Oil comes from millions of marine creatures (called plankton) that died yonks ago. Each individual speck of dead plankton was made of a mixture of hydrogen and carbon — the same as most living matter.

Buried very deep and for a very long time, heat and pressure changed the organisms into oil and gas. This floated up (very, very slowly) before becoming trapped in the rocks.

Oil has been found underneath the North Sea, for instance, but there is lots more waiting to be discovered.

Gas — more than a load of hot air

Rocky's new house will have gas central heating and a gas fire. But where does the gas come from?

Many years ago, when houses and streets were lit by gas, gas was produced from coal. Today, Britain's supply is natural gas and comes in pipes from the North Sea.

Like coal and oil, gas makes lots of by-products that find their way into the house, mainly as plastics.

For peat's sake

Peat is coal 'in the making' and can be burned in the same way.

It is soft and can be cut with a knife

Up until now, Rocky had looked for geological clues outside the home and had used a hand lens to examine some of the naturally occurring rocks and artificial stone found there. The notebook was already becoming full of scribbled notes.

You can see part of it on the back page.

But my house looks BORING

Rocky liked being a scientific detective. 'The outside is really interesting — so what sort of clues will I find on the inside?' Rocky wondered. It was time to peep inside.

'There's hardly anything here! It's boring! All I can see are plugs and sockets, walls covered in plaster, a fireplace in the lounge and paint almost everywhere — including spots on the floor. What a mess. But are there any clues... what is paint, anyway?'

What is paint?

Paint is a mixture of fillers *(extenders that spread the colour out)* and colour *(pigment)*.

The most widely used extender is calcium carbonate — which comes from chalk, limestone or marble. This is used mainly in undercoats and emulsion paints. Paints may also contain two other extenders, china clay (kaolin) and talc, which make the paint thick and sticky.

Ingredients like alumina and silica or antimony, zinc and zirconium are used to make the paint shiny but colour comes from pigments like titanium dioxide (white) and iron oxide (shades of red and brown)

'I remember iron oxide!' Rocky exclaimed. 'It's the bits of rusty iron used to colour concrete roof tiles.'

Plastics are sometimes added to paint, especially for use outdoors, to protect it against the weather and make it last a long time.

What about wallpaper?

Wallpaper is mainly coloured with vegetable dyes which are cheerful and harmless.

But they were not always so harmless. In 1775, the Swedish chemist Karl Wilhelm Scheele created 'Scheele's green'. It contained arsenic — one of the favourite poisons in murder mysteries — an element that is found in some types of rock.

The cheap, bright pigment was welcomed by the industry of the day and widely used in paints, fabrics and wallpapers.

Deadly decorations

There may have been some truth in the author and playwright Oscar Wilde declaring on his death bed that 'this wallpaper is killing me'. It might have been Scheele's green or copper arsenite.

Napoleon, too, may have been accidentally poisoned by being imprisoned at St Helena in rooms decorated with a wallpaper containing the same deadly substance.

They only realised the danger when hundreds of people became ill — they were suffering from arsenic poisoning.

'This wallpaper is killing me'

Rocky wondered what it was made of...

Plastic — and what else?

Rocky noticed that even though the house was not yet furnished, there was plastic all over the place. Window frames, doors, electric light fittings and even a mug left behind by one of the workers were made of plastic.

Plastic is useful because it is light in weight, cheap to produce, strong and colourful.

However, the new bath was <u>not</u> plastic. It was made of a different substance altogether. It was hard and shiny.

'I wonder what it's made of,' thought Rocky, hitting it gently. It sounded like metal. 'There's a good reason for that, 'Rocky thought. 'It's made of metal.'

The bath was made from galvanised steel coated with clay minerals and enamelled to produce a surface that is resistant to scratching.

Galvanised steel is made from a mixture of tin, coke and ironstone — dipped into zinc to protect it from rusting.

Looking for geological clues around the new house, Rocky peered very closely at the fireplace in the lounge. There were certain to be some different kinds of rocks or minerals there as well as reconstituted rock *(leftover pieces glued back together again)* that was cheaper than the real thing.

It was useful to look. And it was useful to get an idea of the feel and sound, too. So Rocky rested a hand on it. It felt cool and sounded solid and dense.

What is plastic anyway?

Rocky found out that plastic is made from oil, gas and coal by boiling off (or distilling). The residue left behind is then used to make all plastics.

Can you name things made of plastic?
Some ideas are given below (upside down, just to be difficult).

- cling-film used to cover food
- the shells of fridges and freezers
- heat-resistant work tops
- the water tank in the roof
- all those buckets and bowls

The white marble was interesting, seen through the hand lens. It was quite different to the other materials used in the new house — there were more than enough clues to fill the notebook.

But Rocky was now exhausted. It had been an exciting day.

'It all begins again tomorrow,' Rocky thought. 'when the removal van comes with all the bits and pieces for the house. With the curtains and the furniture and the cooker and the fridge and the crockery and the cat ... the cat...?'

What has the cat got to do with geology? ... yawn... it had been a long and tiring day.

'Being an 'ologist', Rocky thought, 'is not a lazy job. But it is hungry work...'

Dad,

dad,

dad, can I have geology for dinner?

It sounds as if Rocky is joking. But isn't it true? What about salt, for example? Dinner would be dull without a little bit of sodium chloride. And there is calcium carbonate, which is used in making bread, biscuits, cakes, sweets and ice cream... and titanium dioxide and oxides of aluminium, silver, iron and gold are also used to colour or preserve food. ('Even this bag of sweets ..' murmured Rocky, through a mouthful of crunchy bits.)

And they all come from rocks... Like almost everything else, it seems... but that's another story...

Building from basics *is written by:*
Dr Brian J Taylor and
Hilary J Heason AMIPR
Illustrated by Noel Ford

This book is based on an exhibition entitled 'Geology & You', produced by the British Geological Survey about the geology of the domestic house.
It is, therefore, dedicated to the late Linda Wahl.

We acknowledge the help of colleagues Michael Price, David Highley, Andrew Bloodworth and Chris Green.

Technical assistance came from David Wilson Homes (North Midlands) Ltd, ICI Paints plc and British Glass Technology Ltd.

We are indebted to the many schools (too numerous to detail) who gave input and advice.

Photographs from the British Geological Survey's collection.

Printed in England for the British Geological Survey by Clearpoint Colour Print, Nottingham. C100

ROCKY'S NOTEBOOK

AGGREGATE – BROKEN STONE, SAND AND GRAVEL ETC. BONDED TOGETHER BY CEMENT TO FORM CONCRETE

CONTOURS – LINES ON A MAP JOINING POINTS OF EQUAL HEIGHT OR ALTITUDE. COMPILED BY ORDNANCE SURVEY

CORE (OF ROCK) – THE SOLID CYLINDER OR STICK OF ROCK CUT AND BROUGHT TO THE SURFACE BY DRILLING

ELEMENTS – THESE CANNOT BE DIVIDED INTO SIMPLER SUBSTANCES. OVER 100 EXIST IN NATURE

EVAPORATE – LOSE WATER AS VAPOUR

FOLD – A BEND IN ROCKS, LIKE PUSHING A TABLE CLOTH FROM BOTH ENDS

FRACTURE – A BREAK OR FAULT IN ROCKS (LIKE A 'FRACTURED LEG)

GEOTHERMAL ENERGY – ENERGY FROM THE EARTH LIKE HOT ROCKS AND HOT WATER

HOT' ROCKS – ROCKS (E.G. GRANITE) HEATED FROM WITHIN BY RADIOACTIVE ELEMENTS

IGNEOUS – ROCK THAT WAS ORIGINALLY VERY HOT BUT LATER COOLED INTO A CRYSTALLINE MASS

IMPERMEABLE ROCKS – THESE PREVENT WATER OR ANY OTHER FLUID PASSING THROUGH THEM

INSULATION – A PROCESS THAT HELPS TO PREVENT HEAT OR SOUND ESCAPING FROM ONE MATERIAL TO THE NEXT